Henry David Thoreau

Civil Disobedience

Derek Miller

Cavendish Square
New York

Published in 2018 by Cavendish Square Publishing, LLC
243 5th Avenue, Suite 136, New York, NY 10016

First Edition

Cataloging-in-Publication Data

Names: Miller, Derek.
Title: Henry David Thoreau: civil disobedience / Derek Miller.
Description: New York : Cavendish Square, 2018. | Series: Peaceful protesters | Includes index.
Identifiers: ISBN 9781502631121 (library bound) | ISBN 9781502633941 (Paperback) I ISBN 9781502631138 (ebook)
Subjects: LCSH: Thoreau, Henry David, 1817-1862. Civil disobedience. | Thoreau, Henry David, 1817-1862--Political and social views. | Politics and literature--United States--History--19th century.
Classification: LCC PS3051.C5 M52 2018 | DDC 818'.309--dc23

Editorial Director: David McNamara
Editor: Caitlyn Miller
Copy Editor: Nathan Heidelberger
Associate Art Director: Amy Greenan
Designer: Alan Sliwinski
Production Coordinator: Karol Szymczuk
Photo Research: J8 Media

The photographs in this book are used by permission and through the courtesy of: Cover, pp. 2, 4, 26, 44 Hulton Archive/Getty Images; Background image, ilolab/Shutterstock.com; pp. 11, 18 Everett Historical/Shutterstock.com; p. 13 Craig Stock Arts/Shutterstock.com; p. 28 Internet Archive Book Images/File: A brief history of the nations and of their progress in civilization (1896) (14595765389).jpg/Wikimedia Commons; p. 30 Photo Researchers/Getty Images; p. 32 Muhgcee/File: San Antonio Texas Alamo.JPG/Wikimedia Commons; p. 35 Public Domain/File: James K. Polk portrait.png/Wikimedia Commons; p. 39 The White House Historical Association, Gift of Mrs. Betty Taylor Dandridge/File: Zachary Taylor by Joseph Henry Bush, c1848.jpg/Wikimedia Commons; p. 40 Kballen/File: Mexican Cession.png/Wikimedia Commons; p. 46 Brian Stansberry/File:Jail-cells-moa-tn1.jpg/Wikimedia Commons; p. 49 © North Wind Picture Archives; p. 50 sjbooks/Alamy Stock Photo; p. 63 Public Domain/File: John-brown 000000ac.jpg/Wikimedia Commons; p. 64 Frank Leslie's illustrated newspaper, v. 8, no. 205 (1859 Nov. 5), p. 359/File: John Brown interior engine house.jpg / Wikimedia Commons; p. 70 JHU Sheridan Libraries/Gado/Getty Images; p. 74 Central Press/Hulton Archive/Getty Images; p. 77 Library of Congress, Prints & Photographs/File: Leo Tolstoy 1897, 37767u.jpg/Wikimedia Commons; p. 79 www.photographersdirect.com/File: Franz Roubaud. Count Argutinsky crossing the Caucasian range, 1892.jpg/Wikimedia Commons; p. 82 Library of Congress Prints & Photographs/File: CountTolstoyWifeSonAndDog.187090.ws.jpg/Wikimedia Commons; p. 84 Author unknown/File: Mohandas K. Gandhi, portrait.jpg/Wikimedia Commons; p. 90 Don Cravens/The LIFE Images Collection/Getty Images; p. 91 Bettmann Archive/Getty Images.

Printed in China

Contents

ONE Who Was Henry David Thoreau? 5

TWO War and Slavery 19

THREE Nonviolent Resistance 47

FOUR The Effects of Civil Disobedience 75

Chronology 98

Glossary 100

Further Information 103

Bibliography 105

Index 109

About the Author 112

"Under a government which imprisons any unjustly, the true place for a just man is also a prison." –Henry David Thoreau

CHAPTER ONE

Who Was Henry David Thoreau?

Few figures defined the history of the twentieth century as much as Martin Luther King Jr. and Mahatma Gandhi. Their names call to mind peace and justice to this day, decades after their deaths, and children still study their words and actions in schools around the world. In times of extreme brutality—soon after World War II and the Holocaust and, later, the Vietnam War—Gandhi and King used peace instead of violence to change the world and improve the lives of millions of people. But they did not invent the peaceful means of protest that they made famous.

It was the words of Henry David Thoreau, a figure of much less fame than King and Gandhi, that they both turned to for inspiration in their struggles. A rather eccentric American writer and philosopher, Thoreau lived during the nineteenth century. Although he is perhaps best known for his modest lifestyle and love of nature, Thoreau was deeply concerned about the political order of his day. His chief concerns were the issues of slavery, which he abhorred, and the Mexican-American War, which he viewed as a war of American aggression. To protest these issues, he refused to pay his poll tax of $1.50 (equal to about $45 in 2017). Nothing came of his decision for a number of years, until one summer day in 1846.

In July of that year, Henry David Thoreau walked into Concord, Massachusetts, from his hut on the outskirts of town. He happened to meet the local tax collector, a man by the name of Sam Staples. Staples asked that Thoreau pay his taxes. Thoreau refused. In an act of kindness, Staples then offered to pay the tax himself if Thoreau did not have the money to do so. Thoreau once again refused, saying that he did so out of principle rather than for lack of money. Left with little choice, Staples escorted Thoreau to jail. The next morning, Staples went to the jail and released Thoreau (who was reluctant to leave) and told him that someone else had paid the tax on his behalf.

The events of those two days might have remained a somewhat strange story relegated to a sleepy corner of New England were it not for an essay that Thoreau published three years later. In the essay, "Resistance to Civil Governance" (now known as "**Civil Disobedience**"), Thoreau denounces the American government and urges people to withdraw their support from a government that sanctions the evils of slavery and a war of aggression on Mexico. He says people should refuse to pay their taxes and not be silent witnesses to injustice. His words would not inspire a peaceful resolution to the question of slavery—that debate would be settled on the battlefields of the Civil War. But his words did inspire later generations of peaceful reformers to refuse to cooperate with unjust governments and to use nonviolent means to bring about change. In this way, Thoreau's night in jail came to influence people around the world including both King and Gandhi, among others.

Early Life

The man who came to be known as Henry David Thoreau was born as David Henry Thoreau in Concord in 1817. Concord was a small town at the time, located about 20 miles (32.2 kilometers) from the much larger city of Boston. Thoreau spent almost all of his life there, delighting in the natural surroundings of the town as well as the company of intellectuals who called it home. Thoreau's family was one of some means but not especially wealthy. His father owned a small business that manufactured pencils, and this supported the family. His mother was an **abolitionist** who helped organize the transit of escaped slaves by opening her home to them. Thoreau had three siblings, but he was closest to his older brother, John, who played a central role in Thoreau's life for many years.

Thoreau's childhood was uneventful. He was a thoughtful, serious child, so much so that his nickname was "the judge." However, he delighted in spending time in the forest—even at a young age, his love of nature was apparent. He also excelled in school, and this led his relatives to scrape together enough money to pay for his tuition to college.

In 1833, Thoreau entered Harvard University (then called Harvard College). He was forced at one point to drop out of school due to financial and health difficulties. However, he returned the next semester and graduated from Harvard in 1837. He was a middling student there, graduating in the top half of his class but not excelling to any extraordinary degree. When he returned home from Harvard, he began to call himself "Henry David Thoreau" rather than his given name of "David Henry Thoreau." This peculiar habit confused the people of the town and no doubt contributed to his reputation as an odd fellow.

After graduating, he became a teacher at a school in Concord. However, his tenure there was quite short. Two weeks after the start of the school year, a member of the school committee observed that Thoreau was not using corporal punishment (physical punishment), even though his class was noisier than it should have been. He instructed Thoreau to use corporal punishment to enforce discipline. To underscore the ridiculousness of this demand, Thoreau chose several students at random and struck their hands with a ferule (a rod of wood used for this purpose). That same day, Thoreau resigned his position rather than continue to teach and mete out punishment to his students.

It turned out that his resignation may have been overly hasty. The country was in the midst of an economic depression, and Thoreau struggled to find another teaching position. For close to a year he searched fruitlessly, sending letters around the country and touring Maine in search of a school that was hiring. He and his brother, John, even considered moving out west to Kentucky to try to find jobs, but before they departed, John found one closer to home. Finally, Thoreau started his own private school in Concord, at first in the Thoreau family home and later in an old schoolhouse. This venture was successful enough that Thoreau's brother soon quit his own teaching job to join him. Before long, they had met their goal of twenty-five pupils; life seemed good. They took their students on nature walks, and Thoreau tried to impart his love for the natural world to them.

However, everything would soon fall apart. John became ill, and Thoreau was forced to close down the school since he could not run it on his own. A short time later, John cut his thumb while shaving and developed lockjaw (now more commonly known as tetanus). The infection results in muscle spasms that often occur in the jaw and give the disease its name. John did not recover. After a painful period of illness, he passed away in his brother's arms. His death devastated Thoreau.

Once more out of work, Thoreau went to work in his father's pencil factory. He turned his intellect toward improving the family business and developing new processes to make higher-quality pencils. But Thoreau was not ready to settle down and live an ordinary life going to work each day. Since graduating from Harvard, he had struck up a friendship with the most prominent resident of Concord: Ralph Waldo Emerson. Emerson was a famous author at the time, and Thoreau's reputation never matched that of Emerson's during his life. He took a job as Emerson's handyman, living in his house and helping out around the property. Emerson regarded the younger Thoreau as an intellectual equal, and they spent many hours conversing. Thoreau also gained access to Emerson's considerable library, and their friendship had a profound effect on both of their lives.

Transcendentalism

Ralph Waldo Emerson was the most famous American intellectual of his time.

The story of the lives of Emerson and Thoreau is bound up with the transcendentalist movement of the time. Transcendentalism was a literary and philosophical movement that began in 1836 with the founding of the Transcendental Club. Emerson was a founding member and the unquestioned leader of the movement. He was its most famous member, and he championed its causes.

The transcendentalist movement is difficult to categorize or pin down. Indeed, one of the main tenets that united its members was their belief in the power of the individual, rather than the power of a group or religious organization. They stressed self-reliance and original thought, as well as a deep respect for and admiration of the natural world. The group was also united by its rejection of some popular Christian ideas of the age. Notably, they found fault in the argument that the tenets of Christianity were proven fact due to the witnessing of miracles in biblical times. Transcendentalists did not believe this line of thinking was convincing. They also doubted the infallibility of the Bible, which put them at odds with many of their Christian countrymen. Their assertion that the Bible was not the perfect word of God was due to the work of other intellectuals at the time who realized that the Bible was authored by many different people over a long period.

Of the many members of the transcendentalist movement, Thoreau and Emerson have enjoyed by far the greatest fame throughout history. Although during their lives Thoreau was often seen as a hanger-on of Emerson rather than an intellectual in his own right, his reputation grew after his death. Yet though the friendship between Thoreau and Emerson was quite deep for a time, it would not last forever. They gradually had a falling out, the exact cause of which is still debated. It likely had roots in Thoreau's somewhat difficult personality, as well as Emerson's failure to review or support one of Thoreau's publications.

Whatever the cause, their relationship soured over time. Soon after Thoreau's death, a contemporary reported that Emerson had said to her, "Henry often reminded me of an animal in human form. He had the eye of a bird, the scent of a dog, the most acute, delicate intelligence—but no soul. No, Henry could not have had a human soul."

Today, Walden Pond State Reservation hosts visitors from around the world.

Walden Pond

Despite its rocky end, Thoreau's friendship with Emerson led to one of the most important chapters in Thoreau's life. In 1845, he asked Emerson to allow him to build a hut on Emerson's land near Walden Pond so that Thoreau could live there quietly surrounded by nature. Emerson agreed, and Thoreau went into the woods to live a life largely apart from society. He lived there with very little, spending no more than was required. In all, his cabin cost just $28.12 (roughly $860 in 2017) for him to build—most of which was spent on boards, bricks, and shingles that he carried to the site himself. He would spend more than two years at

Walden Pond. As a result of his time there, he published one of his most important works, ***Walden***.

In *Walden,* Thoreau describes his reasons for living in the woods:

> "
>
> *I went to the woods because I wished to live deliberately, to front only the essential facts of life, and see if I could not learn what it had to teach, and not, when I came to die, discover that I had not lived. I did not wish to live what was not life, living is so dear; nor did I wish to practice resignation, unless it was quite necessary. I wanted to live deep and suck out all the marrow of life, to live so sturdily and Spartan-like as to put to rout all that was not life, to cut a broad swath and shave close, to drive life into a corner, and reduce it to its lowest terms, and, if it proved to be mean, why then to get the whole and genuine meanness of it, and publish its meanness to the world; or if it were sublime, to know it by experience, and be able to give a true account of it in my next excursion.*

Walden is a diverse work that has influenced a great number of people and movements in history who have all interpreted it in their own way. It is a startling rejection of both society and materialism, as well as a call to move closer to nature and to more closely examine ourselves and our world. All in all, it is remembered as one of the most important works of the era in American literature, even though its reputation was more controversial at the time.

Personality

Mainly as a result of his withdrawal from society and the voluntary poverty that he described in *Walden*, Thoreau's personality has come under repeated attack. Critics in his own time and even today delight in calling Thoreau a misanthrope—a hater of all mankind—a self-indulgent loner, and a smug puritan who felt superior because he neither drank alcohol nor ate meat.

His contemporaries wrote about him with little sympathy. The author Nathaniel Hawthorne, who wrote *The Scarlet Letter*, wrote to a friend regarding Thoreau, "You would find him well worth knowing; he is a man of thought and originality, with a certain iron-pokerish-ness, an uncompromising stiffness in his mental character, which is interesting, though it grows rather wearisome on close and frequent acquaintance." After Thoreau's death, another famous author, Robert Louis Stevenson, summed up some of the reasons for the passionate hatred of the man, including quotations from Emerson on the subject:

> *"He was bred to no profession," says Emerson; "he never married; he lived alone; he never went to church; he never voted; he refused to pay a tax to the State; he ate no flesh, he drank no wine, he never knew the use of tobacco and, though a naturalist, he used neither trap nor gun. When asked at dinner what dish he preferred, he answered, 'the nearest.'" So many negative superiorities begin to smack a little of the* ***prig****. From his later works he was in the habit of cutting out the humorous passages, under the impression that they were beneath the dignity of his moral muse; and there we see the prig stand public and confessed.*

However, such criticisms neglect the complicated personality of Thoreau. Those who knew him recalled that he often sought out company—contrary to how he was portrayed, sometimes even by himself—and was a kind, gentle man. In fact, one of those students who was beaten by Thoreau when Thoreau was a teacher later recalled, "When I went to my seat, I was so mad that I said to myself, 'When I'm grown up, I'll whip you for this, old feller.' But I never saw the day I wanted to do it.—Why Henry Thoreau was the kindest hearted of men."

Later Years

After leaving Walden Pond in 1846, Thoreau spent most of his remaining years in Concord. He traveled widely throughout the Northeast and neighboring area, going to Maine as well as Chicago. But most of his time was spent close to home, surrounded by the natural world he so dearly loved. He made a living as a land surveyor; however, he never devoted substantial time to jobs for money. Instead, he observed the world around him and wrote many works on natural history.

It was also in these last sixteen years of his life that Thoreau published his most famous works: "Civil Disobedience" in 1849, *Walden* in 1854, and his later abolitionist writings. These cemented his place in the American literary tradition, inspired people for many generations, and continue to influence people today.

Thoreau had suffered from tuberculosis for most of his life after becoming infected in 1835. Yet his health was relatively stable until he contracted bronchitis in 1859. At that point, it became clear that he would never fully recover. He ultimately lived for three more years, until his death in 1862. He expressed no fear of his impending death, and according to accounts, he passed away peacefully without anxiety. His tombstone bears just one word: "Henry."

Conditions in slave ships were inhumane, and many Africans died during the journey.

CHAPTER TWO

War and Slavery

Thoreau's peaceful protest through his refusal to pay taxes focused on two issues: slavery and the Mexican-American War. He was not alone in his concern over these issues at the time. There was a deep political divide in the country with regard to both issues. Democrats were mostly proslavery and expansionist, while Whigs were mostly antislavery and against the war with Mexico. What set Thoreau apart was his insistence that men should not stand idly by as the majority set the policy of the nation when that policy was so clearly unjust. But before we take an in-depth view at Thoreau's thoughts on this subject, it is necessary to look at the historical background of the time.

The history of the United States is inextricably connected to the institution of slavery. It played an integral part in the economy throughout the nation's time as a colony and as a newly independent state. The controversy of slavery—which was recognized as morally questionable from its early days—was a constant source of tension in the history of the United States. Progressive thinkers such as Thoreau (among many others) saw the evils of slavery clearly, and they denounced its practice. However, it proved difficult to stop the practice, and it was not until after the Civil War that it finally came to an end.

Slavery Comes to the New World

The first permanent English settlement in North America was Jamestown. Founded in 1607 after earlier failures to establish a foothold on the vast continent, Jamestown was the capital of Virginia for close to a century. Jamestown is where enslaved Africans were first brought to what would later become the United States. Dutch traders sold twenty men to the colonists in 1619—just twelve years after the colony was established.

Soon, the American institution of slavery had taken root in the new British colonies. The colonies desperately needed a source of labor to produce more goods—primarily tobacco—and relatively few Europeans were willing to make the dangerous sea voyage to labor in appalling conditions. A small number of indentured servants—Europeans who agreed to work for a number of years in exchange for passage to the New World—did such work, but their numbers were not sufficient. It was for this reason that the institution of slavery began in Virginia and spread across North America. Due to economic considerations, slavery took deeper root in the Southern colonies. New England farms did not require the huge labor supply that Southern tobacco plantations needed. While there were slaves in the Northern colonies at this point, they were not vital to the region's economy.

In these early days, the institution of slavery was formalized and took shape. It was determined that African slaves would live their entire life in bondage—unlike indentured servants. They and their children would live lives as "property" rather than as men and women with the rights inherent to human beings. As a result, they were often horribly mistreated. They could be beaten and whipped by their masters, and families were routinely separated when slave owners decided to sell children for profit or to separate wives and husbands for convenience.

The Birth of the United States

Perhaps the most important day in American history is July 4, 1776, the day that the Declaration of Independence was adopted by the thirteen colonies. The United States was born as the world's newest nation. The document signed that day was a rallying call for democratic rule and human rights. It includes some of the most famous words in history, which have inspired people around the world:

> “
>
> *We hold these truths to be self-evident, that all men are created equal, that they are endowed by their Creator with certain unalienable Rights, that among these are Life, Liberty and the pursuit of Happiness.*

It was a noble vision, but one that even the authors knew they were betraying. Thomas Jefferson, the author of the Declaration of Independence, originally included a paragraph that denounced King George. He wrote:

> “
>
> *He has waged cruel war against human nature itself, violating its most sacred rights of life and liberty in the persons of a distant people who never offended him, captivating and carrying them into slavery in another hemisphere or to incur miserable death in their transportation thither.*

However, this was cut from the final draft at the insistence of delegates from Southern states. It also does not betray the fact that Jefferson himself was a slave owner—an inconvenient truth that shows the conflicted feelings toward slavery at the time. Jefferson was a constant critic of slavery throughout his life (writing at one point it was a "moral depravity"), though he was an owner of hundreds of slaves.

The Founding Fathers were aware of their hypocrisy. While there was little doubt that slavery would exist in their new country due to the economic benefits it provided both farmers in the South and businessmen in the North, they avoided using the word "slave" in the Constitution to avoid the appearance of federal support for slavery. The issue of slavery would ultimately come up three times in the Constitution. The first instance is in the three-fifths compromise, which states that a single slave is calculated as three-fifths of a person for the purposes of calculating representatives and taxes. Through fanciful phrasing, the authors of the compromise managed to do this without ever using the word "slave," referring to "all other persons" outside of "free Persons, including those bound to Service for a Term of Years, and excluding Indians not taxed." The second instance is the fugitive slave clause, which demands the return of a "Person held to Service or Labour" back to the "Party to whom such Service or Labour may be due," even if they cross a state line. This clause proved important in later debates concerning slavery because of the feeling in the South that it was not enforced strictly enough.

The third instance regards the Atlantic slave trade and reads, "The Migration or Importation of such Persons as any of the States now existing shall think proper to admit shall not be prohibited by the Congress prior to the Year one thousand eight hundred and eight." This was an important compromise between antislavery and proslavery politicians that says the importing of slaves could not be banned until at least 1808. On the one hand, politicians from the South believed that they could likely defeat any measure to ban the slave trade in twenty years' time. On the other, politicians from the North argued that it offered hope for a ban of the slave trade, something that was not possible at all before the Constitution came into effect. For these opposing reasons, politicians on both sides agreed to sign the Constitution.

In this way, the stage was set for further conflict over the question of slavery. The Founding Fathers had managed to paper over the deep rift that slavery was causing in the country to forge a lasting Constitution, but they were unable to settle the question definitively. Over time, opponents and proponents of slavery only grew increasingly militant and unwilling to compromise.

North and South

Around the time of the American Revolution, people in the North and South of the country began to see slavery very differently. In the North, slavery was never a cornerstone of the local economy. Tobacco and cotton production never took place on a large scale due to the cold climate. Therefore, people in the North were much more sympathetic to the plight of slaves and were willing to outlaw slavery completely. In the South, the local economy was utterly dependent on cheap labor—first for tobacco production and later for cotton production. The system of large plantations and labor-intensive crops made slavery much more lucrative than in the North.

These economic differences that arose from different climates made the South the defender of slavery, while the North began to turn against it on moral grounds. By 1804, slavery was abolished throughout the North. At one time, it seemed possible that slavery might meet the same fate in the South, as it became less and less lucrative to own slaves. However, this changed in 1793 with Eli Whitney's invention of the cotton gin. The cotton gin allowed cotton to be prepared for textile production much for efficiently than before. This in turn set off a manufacturing boom around the world as producing cotton garments became much more profitable. The end result was that slavery

The use of slave labor to pick cotton—a backbreaking job—made growing cotton highly profitable.

became more lucrative than ever before. The demand for slaves skyrocketed throughout the South, and the demand for cotton in the North silenced a great deal of criticism of slavery.

A Delicate Balance

Nevertheless, despite the economic advantages of slavery, opposition to slavery continued to grow and became a heated political issue on the national stage. Opinions became more and more divided in the United States. Yet there was a delicate balance of power that prevented proslavery or antislavery camps from accomplishing much: there were eleven Free States and eleven slave states. This system was threatened in 1819, when Missouri (then a territory) petitioned to become a slave state. If the petition were granted, the balance would tip, and slave states would outnumber Free States. To prevent such a situation, a deal was struck by the opposing factions: the **Missouri Compromise**. Missouri would be admitted as a slave state, but Maine would also be admitted as a Free State (it had been part of Massachusetts up until this point in history). The compromise also tried to settle the issue of how to handle new states in the West being admitted to the United States. Any state north of the 36°30′ latitude line, with the exception of Missouri, would be a Free State, while any state south of the line would be a slave state.

This worked for a time, until Kansas petitioned to become a state in 1854. Kansas was north of the 36°30′ latitude line and therefore should have been a Free State. However, Southern lawmakers were unwilling to tip the balance of power in the favor of the favor of the Free States. They simply blocked the admission of Kansas. While abolitionists and Northern politicians railed against the betrayal of the Missouri Compromise, they could do nothing other than create a new deal to win over Southern votes. The result was the **Kansas-Nebraska Act** of 1854.

Two new states were created instead of just one. But rather than the federal government deciding if they were Free States or slave states, settlers in the newly formed territories would vote to decide whether or not slavery would be allowed. This new policy was called **popular sovereignty**, and it had disastrous results. Not only did it cause outrage in the North because it violated

As the United States expanded, the issue of slavery became more and more contentious.

the Missouri Compromise, it also led to bloodshed in the West in a conflict known as Bleeding Kansas.

Fanatics both for and against slavery flocked to the new territories to try to influence the vote. Tensions grew as armed groups entered Kansas from the North and South. On May 21, 1856, the town of Lawrence was sacked by a proslavery group, and the violence soon spread. Three days later, an abolitionist by the name of John Brown gathered a group of men and visited the house of a proslavery neighbor in the settlement of Pottawatomie Creek. Brown and his men took three men outside and murdered them savagely in cold blood. They continued on to two more houses, killing two more men with their swords and guns. The events of that night would come to be known as the **Pottawatomie Massacre**, and they sparked more conflict in Kansas. John Brown evaded justice, but his story was not over. As we will see later, he had a much larger part to play in American history.

The Dred Scott Case

Violence in Kansas gradually came to an end. However, it was just a warning of the violence that would soon come to engulf the entire nation with the Civil War. But before that point, there remained another attempt to settle the issue of slavery once and for all and prevent more violence. This time, it was the Supreme Court that tried to intervene, not Congress.

A slave by the name of Dred Scott petitioned a Missouri court that he be freed on the grounds that he had lived in Free States with his master for some time before returning to Missouri. The **Dred Scott case** was a case like many others before it, but it quickly became extraordinary as it was appealed all the way to the Supreme Court. In a decision that would later come to be known as one of the worst in American history, the Supreme Court shocked the country. Seven of nine justices ruled that Dred Scott could not even petition the court on the basis that he was black and all blacks—whether enslaved or free—were not

In 1857, despite the Supreme Court decision, Dred Scott was emancipated by his owner. He died the next year from tuberculosis.

American citizens. Furthermore, the court ruled that the federal government had no authority to outlaw slavery in its territories and new states. In other words, slavery was legal throughout the West, and the long history of compromise on the issue was, in fact, unconstitutional. Abolitionists around the country were horrified. With the stroke of a pen, slavery had swept across the country, and African Americans—even those who were not slaves—were stripped of citizenship and the rights that came with it.

Contrary to the wishes of the court, the ruling did not settle the issue of slavery and prevent further conflict. Instead, it outraged abolitionists and Northern lawmakers, some of whom came to believe that violence represented the only way forward. Just four years later, eleven states seceded and left the United States, triggering the American Civil War, a conflict that definitively settled the question of slavery with the emancipation of all African Americans—at the cost, by some estimates, of more than seven hundred thousand American lives.

The Texas Revolution

Slavery was not the only injustice that concerned Thoreau. The Mexican-American War, fought between 1846 and 1848, also attracted his criticism. To understand the war, it is necessary to look much further back in the past to the roots of the conflict. In 1821, Mexico won its independence

Today, the Alamo is a popular tourist attraction in Texas.

from Spain—the colonial power that ruled it for centuries in much the same way that Great Britain ruled the United States before the American Revolution. Mexico at that time was a sprawling country, encompassing not just modern-day Mexico but also much of what is now the western United States (including the states of California, Texas, Nevada, Arizona, and Utah). Problematically for Mexico, much of this land that is now part of the United States was virtually unsettled. It was inhabited by Native Americans, who did not think of themselves as citizens of Mexico.

As a result, Mexico tried to encourage immigration to these regions, especially the province of Tejas (which later became Texas). This measure proved successful, and thousands of Americans poured into the area to take advantage of offers of cheap land. They brought their slaves with them, and although Mexico tried to ban slavery, little changed in Tejas, far from the capital of Mexico City. Mexico sought to stem the flood of American immigration, but it was too late. By 1832, there were an estimated 30,000 Anglo-Americans in Tejas and just 7,800 Mexicans—as well as thousands of slaves.

In 1835, the American immigrants in Texas rebelled against Mexico, which was ruled by the dictator Antonio López de Santa Anna. At first, the Texan forces beat back the Mexican soldiers who came to quell the revolt. But soon Santa Anna arrived at the head of an army numbering some seven thousand men and advanced toward the city of San Antonio. The Texan defenders, around two hundred soldiers and volunteers, fortified the Alamo Mission and attempted to stop Santa Anna's advance. Texas also declared independence from Mexico during this time. Santa Anna laid siege to the Alamo for thirteen days, demanding its surrender. Then he launched an assault and stormed the mission compound. All the defenders were killed.

After the Alamo, Mexican and Texan forces clashed in the Battle of Coleto. Approximately four hundred Texans were captured after losing the battle. They were all executed by order of Santa Anna at the Goliad Massacre. The situation looked grim for the new Texan state, but that was soon to change.

Santa Anna's army was pursuing a smaller force led by Sam Houston. On April 21, 1836, Houston managed to surprise Santa Anna's army and deliver a decisive defeat. The Texan soldiers shouted "Remember the Alamo" as they defeated the Mexican army—a scene that defines Texan history. The Battle of San Jacinto lasted just eighteen minutes. Nearly a thousand Mexican soldiers were killed or captured, while only nine Texans lost their lives. Santa Anna was captured, and he signed a peace treaty with Texas that ended the war. However, Santa Anna lost power during his captivity, and the new government of Mexico refused to recognize the treaty he signed.

The new Republic of Texas existed as an independent state for the next nine years. During that time, it was occasionally in conflict with Mexico, which never recognized its independence. Most Texans wanted to become part of the United States, but this did not happen as quickly as many people expected it would. President Martin Van Buren did not want to start a war with Mexico over the breakaway province, nor did Northern politicians want to admit another slave state.

President Polk and Manifest Destiny

The situation changed in 1844 when James Polk ran for president on an expansionist platform and won the election. Texas was admitted as a slave state in 1845 with his support. Polk was a believer in **manifest destiny**, the idea that the United States was destined to stretch across all of North America from the Atlantic Ocean in the East to the Pacific Ocean in the West. He envisioned not only the acquisition of Texas, but also that of California and other territories then held by Mexico. This public ambition to own a vast strip of Mexican land did little to improve already strained relations between the two countries.

James Polk entered politics at a young age. He became a congressman at just twenty-nine years old.

After Texas was annexed, Mexico did not declare war on the United States as it had threatened to do in the past. Polk turned his attention to the Oregon Territory, which included modern-day Oregon, Washington, and Idaho, as well as a small part of Canada and other US states. The territory was jointly administered by Great Britain and the United States at that time. Through a combination of tough negotiating tactics and implicit threats of war, Polk secured most of the territory for the United States with the Oregon Treaty of 1846.

Next on Polk's list was California—a trickier problem than Oregon since the United States had no claim on it whatsoever. It had always been part of Mexico since Europeans first divided up the New World. Polk sent a special envoy by the name of John Sidell to negotiate purchasing California from the Mexican government. Unsurprisingly, this did not go well. The president of Mexico seemed willing to negotiate with Sidell and to sell the huge province of California—but he was immediately deposed in a coup d'etat. The new government not only refused to negotiate on the sale of California, it also expressed its desire to see Texas returned to Mexico.

At the time, there was a large strip of land claimed by both Texas (and the United States) and Mexico. Situated between the Rio Grande (the current border) and the Nueces River (now in South Texas), this rather barren stretch of desert led to war. Polk ordered General Zachary

Taylor to lead an army into the Nueces Strip and further the American claim on the land. According to scholar Amy S. Greenburg, this decision was met by skepticism even within the United States military. She writes that a colonel sent on the mission went so far as to write home, "We have not one particle of right to be here … It looks as if the government sent a small force on purpose to bring on a war, so as to have a pretext for taking California and as much of this country as it chooses." The soldier did not have to wait long to see his words match reality. In response to General Taylor's movements, a Mexican army arrived on the opposite bank of the Rio Grande and set up camp. A clash soon occurred when a Mexican cavalry unit crossed the river and General Taylor sent a small unit of American soldiers to meet them. Eleven Americans were killed.

Polk demanded that Congress declare war on Mexico—a war he argued already existed due to Mexican actions and simply needed to be formalized. Southern Democrats were fully behind Polk, but Northern Whigs were not convinced that the war was necessary. However, they were also worried that voting against the war would harm their political fortunes when it was being portrayed as one of self-defense. As a result, few voted against the declaration of war, although the opposition did number former president John Quincey Adams—then a US representative—among them. Abraham Lincoln, then a

US representative, also spoke out against the war. This cost him a great deal of popularity in his home state, and he chose not to run for reelection as a representative as a result.

One of the most vocal critics of the war was Representative Joshua Giddings of Ohio. He belonged to the Whig Party, and he denounced the war throughout its entire course. After the war, he was the only congressman to vote against a resolution thanking General Zachary Taylor (whose popularity won Taylor, himself a Whig, the next presidential election). In the early days of the war, Giddings's words reflect the mood of some critics of Polk's efforts to expand the United States:

> “
>
> *This war is waged against an unoffending people, without just or adequate cause, for the purposes of conquest; with the design to extend slavery; in violation of the Constitution, against the dictates of justice, of humanity, the sentiments of the age in which we live, and the precepts of the religion we profess. I will lend it no aid, no support whatever. I will not bathe my hands in the blood of the people of Mexico, nor will I participate in the guilt of those murders which have been and which will hereafter be committed by our army there. For these reasons I shall vote*

against the bill under consideration and all others calculated to support this war.

The War Itself

General Zachary Taylor

Although outnumbered, General Taylor delivered a series of defeats to the Mexican forces that opposed him. He captured the nearby city of Monterrey after a significant battle with heavy losses on both sides. Other American armies swept through California and New Mexico, securing the territory that the United States wished to annex while facing little resistance.

An army under the command of General Winfield Scott set sail for the port city of Veracruz, which offered the easiest path to the capital of Mexico City. Many of Taylor's men were redirected for this effort, and Scott took Veracruz and marched on toward the capital. However, General Santa Anna—once more in power in Mexico—launched an attack on Taylor's weakened positions. With only five thousand men, Taylor held out against an attacking Mexican army numbering some fourteen thousand men. The Battle of Buena Vista helped to cement Taylor's reputation as a general and greatly increased his popularity at home.

Months later, Scott reached Mexico City and captured it, despite Mexican efforts to defend the city. The war was over. More than thirteen thousand American soldiers had died in the conflict (mostly from disease), and Mexico suffered even heavier losses.

The Treaty of Guadalupe Hidalgo

With the war lost, Mexico agreed to negotiate a peace treaty with the United States, the **Treaty of Guadalupe Hidalgo**. In return for $15 million, Mexico agreed to cede California

Mexico ceded a vast swath of territory to the United States to end the Mexican-American War.

and the territory of New Mexico to the United States. Mexicans living on that land were given the choice of swearing allegiance to the United States or giving up their homes and leaving for what remained of Mexico. Mexico also gave up any claim to Texas and recognized its border as the Rio Grande, ceding the Nueces Strip to Texas. In the end, Mexico lost a third of its territory, and the United States increased its size by approximately a quarter. Polk had kept his campaign promise to gain California and the West for the United States, although tens of thousands of soldiers had died in the process.

The Compromise of 1850

The Mexican-American War led to renewed conflict in the United States concerning slavery. In the opening months of the war, antislavery legislators sought to prevent the creation of more slave states by proposing the **Wilmot Proviso**, which would have banned slavery in all territory gained from the war. Southern lawmakers defeated the proviso in the Senate. The issue of how to handle slavery in the new territory (outside of the slave state Texas) remained unsolved until 1850—two years after the end of the Mexican-American War.

The resolution was a complex political deal known as the Compromise of 1850 (which occurred between the Missouri Compromise of 1820 and the Kansas-Nebraska

JOHN C. CALHOUN

While most history books focus on people who championed the cause of justice, it is easy to forget that many people throughout history have defended the opposite side. One of the most vocal defenders of slavery in American history was John C. Calhoun. His long political career saw him hold the positions of US representative, senator, secretary of state, secretary of war (now defense), and vice president. Throughout all roles, he fought tirelessly to preserve the institution of slavery. In one of his most famous speeches, delivered in 1837, Calhoun argued that slavery ought to be seen as "a positive good" and not an "evil" of necessity. He claimed that slavery actually benefited the slaves themselves, who he imagined lived much better lives than poor laborers in Europe. He also said that slavery was a force for stability—it prevented the conflict that inevitably resulted from the vast gulf between rich and poor.

As a result of these views, Calhoun tried to ensure that slavery would continue into the future. He supported the annexation of Texas—a slave state. But he opposed the Mexican-American War and its territorial gains, fearing that they would undermine slavery and cause more conflict over the issue. Today, he is remembered for the huge impact he had on American politics, and he is often credited as one of the most important congressmen of the first half of the nineteenth century. However, his legacy is haunted by his support for slavery.

Act of 1854). According to the compromise, five separate issues would finally be resolved, some in favor of the proslavery camp and others in favor of the antislavery camp. When lawmakers attempted to pass the bill as a single piece of legislation, it was defeated as both proslavery and antislavery radicals voted against it. However, it was then divided into five smaller bills that were passed individually:

- Texas gave up its claims on large portions of land that now belong to other states, including much of Colorado and New Mexico. In return, the federal government assumed its debt.
- California joined the United States as a Free State.
- The territories of Utah and New Mexico were organized, and the issue of slavery was to be determined by popular sovereignty in both.
- In Washington, DC, the buying and selling of slaves was banned, but slavery itself continued.
- The **Fugitive Slave Act** of 1850 was passed.

Those against slavery could point to victories in the admission of California as a Free State, the shrinking of Texas (a slave state), and the banning of the slave trade in Washington, DC. Meanwhile, proslavery lawmakers prevented the outright banning of slavery in the territories of Utah and New Mexico, and they won the much desired strengthening of fugitive slave legislation.

The Fugitive Slave Act of 1850

The Fugitive Slave Act of 1850 was one of the most important pieces of the compromise. Although the fugitive slave clause in the Constitution had resulted in the Fugitive Slave Act of 1793, proslavery lawmakers considered this legislation toothless by 1850. The Underground Railroad

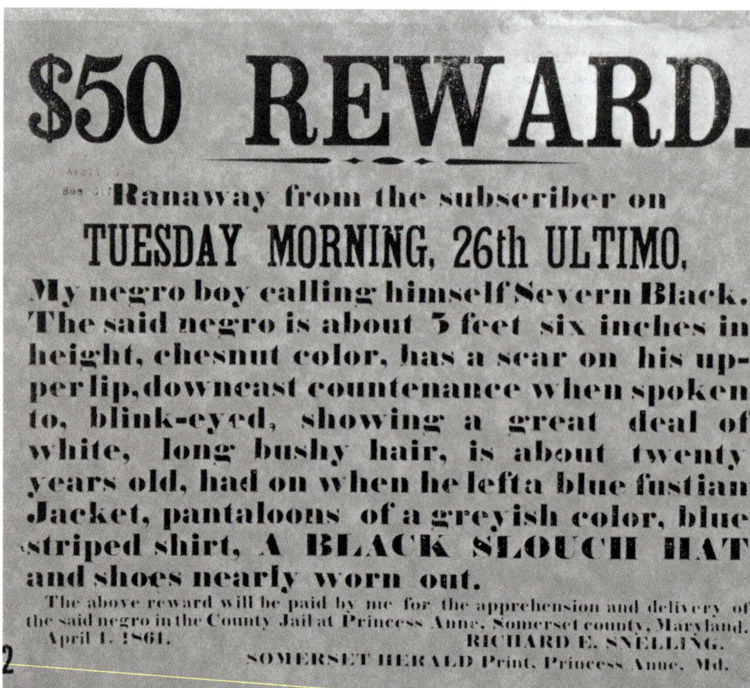

A newspaper advertisement offering a reward for the return of an escaped slave

was spiriting slaves to freedom in the North and Canada, and there was little slave owners could do to stop it. While Northern states were obligated to return these runaway slaves to their masters, they often refused to do so through various means. For instance, runaway slaves were often given jury trials in the North, and juries sometimes ignored the letter of the law in favor of their conscience.

The Fugitive Slave Act of 1850 sought to end such practices. It forbade jury trials for runaway slaves (or free African Americans accused of being runaways). It also greatly increased the penalty for aiding runaway slaves—abolitionists who helped them could face up to a $1,000 fine (almost $30,000 in 2017) and six months in prison. The new law outraged abolitionists and Northern states. Slave catchers were free to roam the North, and those they accused of being runaways had no right to a jury trial to dispute the charge. It inflamed tensions around slavery and served as a rallying call for the abolitionist cause.

Thoreau spent just one night in jail and reported that he was fairly treated there.

CHAPTER THREE

Nonviolent Resistance

If not for slavery and the Mexican-American War, Thoreau may have been content to write little about politics. His extreme individualism did not lend itself to political organizing. But he found himself unable to sit on the sidelines while his country committed terrible acts. In this chapter, we will trace the evolving political views of Thoreau throughout his life. They are at times contradictory; he never tried to present a unified political philosophy. He always looked to the power of the individual to create change.

Thoreau's early writings tend to support **nonviolent resistance**, while his later writings are much more open to violent resistance. Scholars debate whether he radically altered his views over the years, or whether he ever rejected violent resistance in his early writings. Whatever the case may be, Thoreau's legacy is tightly linked to nonviolent resistance. It was his influence on the peaceful protests of Martin Luther King Jr. and Mahatma Gandhi, among others, that cemented his place as an influential political thinker.

Early Career

Thoreau grew up in a household that was devoted to the abolitionist cause. His mother, in particular, was very active in the abolitionist movement, and Thoreau was doubtless exposed to these ideas from a young age. In his early writings, Thoreau appears sympathetic to the plight of slaves, but he does not spend much time discussing them. One of his early essays, "Herald of Freedom," praises a local abolitionist writer; however, Thoreau does not come out and lend his own voice to the cause.

In 1842, Thoreau stopped paying his taxes as a result of his opposition to slavery. This drew little notice at the time. It was four more years before the tax collector confronted Thoreau over his tardiness. Furthermore, Thoreau was in no way the first to protest in this way. Bronson Alcott,

Concord, Massachusetts, was a quiet town during Thoreau's lifetime.

another resident of Concord and the father of Louisa May Alcott, refused to pay his taxes in 1840—two years before Thoreau. Bronson, too, was arrested, though someone else paid the tax on his behalf before he could be imprisoned.

It was in 1846 that Thoreau was finally arrested and imprisoned for his failure to pay his poll tax. He spent just one night in prison. Reportedly, he should not have even spent that long in jail since his tax was paid the same day he was arrested. However, the tax collector received word only after he had returned home and taken off his boots, and he decided not to put them back on and go to the jail. Later critics would sometimes question Thoreau's true devotion to the cause given his short time in jail, although many, like Gandhi, took it as evidence that he was indeed willing to make personal sacrifices.

Thoreau himself seemed disappointed that he was not given the opportunity to spend more time in jail. The sheriff who released him later said that he was "as mad as the devil when I turned him loose."

Thoreau's time in jail was largely uneventful. He got to know his cellmate and was treated well by his guard and fellow prisoners. His friend Emerson came to visit him after receiving word of his arrest. Emerson, himself sympathetic to the abolitionist cause, could not help but ask, "What are you doing in there?" Thoreau responded, "What are you doing out there?" The exchange, reported by Emerson, has been retold time and time again by authors writing about Thoreau. It is a call to action—and a criticism of those who live their lives surrounded by oppression and injustice without fighting for justice and equality.

Thoreau's works are popular to this day.

Civil Disobedience

Undoubtedly, the most important thing to come of Thoreau's incarceration was his political work "Civil Disobedience." First published in 1849, this was Thoreau's first major political writing, and it was inspired by his time spent in jail. The work would inspire civil rights leaders for generations to come—even if it was not especially well known during Thoreau's own lifetime.

It is a deeply critical work that condemns the American government over its support of slavery and the Mexican-American War. Thoreau argues that it is the duty of the individual to cease to support an unjust government. He writes:

> "
>
> *How does it become a man to behave toward this American government today? I answer, that he cannot without disgrace be associated with it. I cannot for an instant recognize that political organization as my government which is the slave's government also.*
>
> *All men recognize the right of revolution; that is, the right to refuse allegiance to, and to resist, the government, when its tyranny or its inefficiency are great and unendurable. But almost all say that such is not the case now. But such was the case, they think, in the [American Revolution]. If one were to tell me that this was a bad government because it taxed certain foreign commodities brought to its ports, it is most probable that I should not make an ado about it, for I can do without them … When a sixth of the population of a nation which has*

undertaken to be the refuge of liberty are slaves, and a whole country is unjustly overrun and conquered by a foreign army, and subjected to military law, I think that it is not too soon for honest men to rebel and revolutionize. What makes this duty the more urgent is the fact that the country so overrun is not our own, but ours is the invading army.

Thoreau is completely uncompromising. In his mind, a government that approves of slavery and a war of aggression cannot be supported. It is immoral to support it in any way, and that includes paying taxes—even when failing to pay them may result in imprisonment.

He viewed slavery as an evil institution that the American government—and people—allowed to persist. He also saw the Mexican-American War as an imperialistic war of aggression that should never have happened. As a result, he repeatedly condemns the actions of the government of the United States, but his criticism does not end there. He takes issue with the very idea of a democratic government, writing:

“

The practical reason why, when the power is once in the hands of the people, a majority are permitted, and for a long period continue, to rule is not because they are most likely to be in the right, nor because this seems fairest to the minority, but because they are physically the strongest. But a government in which the majority rule in all cases cannot be based on justice, even as far as men understand it.

This view that democracy is, in fact, not the ideal form of government may seem strange at first, but the flaws of a democratic system were apparent to Thoreau every day as the institution of slavery persisted without an end in sight. The fact that a majority of Americans did not vocally oppose its existence meant that millions of African Americans lived in deplorable conditions as slaves. The majority was willing to take away African Americans' rights and keep them in bondage for the country's financial benefit and to keep the peace between the North and the South.

In fact, Thoreau is quick to condemn Northerners as much as the Southerners who kept slaves. He writes:

"

Practically speaking, the opponents to a reform in Massachusetts are not a hundred thousand politicians at the South, but a hundred thousand merchants and farmers here, who are more interested in commerce and agriculture than they are in humanity, and are not prepared to do justice to the slave and to Mexico, cost what it may. I quarrel not with far-off foes, but with those who, near at home, cooperate with, and do the bidding of those far away, and without whom the latter would be harmless.

In "Civil Disobedience," Thoreau advocates for nonviolent resistance against the American government. He urges individuals to refuse to pay their taxes and to resign from public office. It is this nonviolent resistance that Thoreau is most remembered for, but later in life he appeared to embrace violent resistance to a much larger degree.

Nonviolent Resistance Before Thoreau

It is important to remember that Thoreau did not invent nonviolent resistance. **Quakers**—who embrace pacifism—had been refusing to pay war taxes for centuries in both Great Britain and the United States. Even within the abolitionist movement of his day, Thoreau was not the first to propose nonviolent resistance. William Lloyd Garrison, one of the most influential New England abolitionists, was devoted to peaceful protest. He completely rejected violent resistance as a hypocritical act. Slavery was evil because violence was used to coerce other human beings. Therefore, attempting to overthrow it through violence was simply replacing one evil with another.

Thoreau the Anarchist?

"Civil Disobedience" also allows a glimpse into Thoreau's political philosophy and his somewhat difficult to classify views in that field. He has often been labeled an **anarchist**—someone who believes the state should be abolished. This view seems clear in "Civil Disobedience," which begins with the words:

> *I heartily accept the motto, "That government is best which governs least"; and I should like to see it acted up to more rapidly and systematically. Carried out, it finally amounts to this, which also I believe—"That government is best which governs not at all"; and when men are prepared for it, that will be the kind of government which they will have.*

Many anarchist thinkers also point to Thoreau's works as an inspiration for their political philosophy. However, Thoreau never called himself an anarchist, and he writes later in "Civil Disobedience," "But, to speak practically and as a citizen, unlike those who call themselves no-government men, I ask for, not at once no government, but at once a better government."

Anti-Militarism

In "Civil Disobedience," Thoreau discusses the military—and the men who serve it—at length. His views are unorthodox and would no doubt earn him a great deal of criticism if they were published today. He savagely condemns those in uniform:

> *A common and natural result of an undue respect for law is, that you may see a file of soldiers, colonel, captain, corporal, privates,* ***powder-monkeys****, and all, marching in admirable order over hill and dale to the wars, against their wills, ay, against their common sense and consciences, which makes it very steep marching indeed, and produces a palpitation of the heart. They have no doubt that it is a damnable business in which they are concerned; they are all peaceably inclined. Now, what are they? Men at all? or small movable forts and magazines, at the service of some unscrupulous man in power?*

In his criticism, it is possible to see his radical views of the importance of the individual. He disparages those in uniform largely because they are no longer capable of acting however they choose. Instead, they are beholden to men in power who order them to do what they are told—whether or not that matches what their own conscience tells them.

Thoreau extends his criticism from those in uniform to all servants of the American government. In a passage unlikely to win him friends, he compares civil servants with pieces of wood, stones, and dogs:

> *The mass of men serve the state thus, not as men mainly, but as machines, with their bodies. They are the standing army, and the militia, jailers, constables,* ***posse comitatus****, etc. In most cases there is no free exercise whatever of the judgment or of the moral sense; but they put themselves on a level with wood and earth and stones; and wooden men can perhaps be manufactured that will serve the purpose as well. Such command no more respect than men of straw or a lump of dirt. They have the same sort of worth only as horses and dogs. Yet such as these even are commonly esteemed good citizens. Others—as most legislators, politicians, lawyers, ministers, and office-holders—serve the state chiefly with their heads; and, as they rarely make any moral distinctions, they are as likely to serve the devil, without intending it.*

In the end, Thoreau is most concerned with the choices of individuals. Agents of the state draw his criticism because they do not make choices for themselves—they simply follow orders. In this way, the ideas of transcendentalism are visible in "Civil Disobedience." The individual—and not the state or larger society—is what matters. People ought to think for themselves, according to Thoreau. Simply bending to the will of the state is not admirable; it is a cause for shame.

Individualism

It is a curious fact that "Civil Disobedience" is so deeply individualistic. Later leaders like Gandhi and King looked to Thoreau's words when leading millions of people. But Thoreau himself always saw his nonviolent resistance as the actions of a single individual, not as part of a greater struggle against injustice. He did not urge other people to resist the government so that the government had to change—he urged them to resist because he thought a moral person had no other choice. Whether or not slavery was abolished as a result was somewhat beside the point. The most important thing was that the individual not stoop to supporting it through his actions. In this way, he differed greatly from the civil rights leaders of later generations, who deeply cared about changing society and not simply about their own individual actions.

Thoreau's views on this matter can be seen clearly in the following passage:

> "
>
> *It is not a man's duty, as a matter of course, to devote himself to the eradication of any, even the most enormous, wrong; he may still properly have other concerns to engage him; but it is his duty, at least, to wash his hands of it, and, if he gives it no thought longer, not to give it practically his support.*

Slavery in Massachusetts

Five years after "Civil Disobedience," Thoreau published his next major political work, "Slavery in Massachusetts." It was based on a speech that he delivered at an antislavery rally. It is an even stronger condemnation of slavery than "Civil Disobedience." It was written four years after the passage of the Fugitive Slave Act of 1850, and the views of New England abolitionists were growing more and more forceful.

In 1854, a runaway slave by the name of Anthony Burns was arrested in Massachusetts. There were massive protests in Boston—a staunchly antislavery city. There was even an armed attempt to free Burns, in which a deputy federal marshal died after being stabbed. But these efforts failed, and a judge in Massachusetts ordered that Burns be returned to his owner in Virginia, as the Fugitive Slave Act required. It was an important moment that inflamed tension in Massachusetts. People who had previously been silent critics of slavery became more and more vocal in the aftermath of the case.

This incident is referenced in Thoreau's essay "Slavery in Massachusetts":

> *The whole military force of the State is at the service of a Mr. Suttle [Burns's master], a slaveholder from Virginia, to enable him to catch a man whom he calls his property; but not a soldier is offered to save a citizen of Massachusetts from being kidnapped!*

Thoreau is deeply critical of his own state, calling for it to leave the United States rather than continue sending escaped slaves back to the South:

> *What should concern Massachusetts is not the Nebraska Bill, nor the Fugitive Slave Bill, but her own slaveholding and servility. Let the State dissolve her union with the slaveholder. She may wriggle and hesitate, and ask leave to*

> *read the Constitution once more; but she can find no respectable law or precedent which sanctions the continuance of such a union for an instant.*
>
> *Let each inhabitant of the State dissolve his union with her, as long as she delays to do her duty.*

It is a radical stance, but not one that was out of place at the time. The rhetoric, both for and against slavery, had reached a feverish intensity by 1854. After the Fugitive Slave Act of 1850, many abolitionists felt that all states were practically slave states, when slave catchers could accost any African American and have him sent South without even a jury trial.

Despite the strong sentiments of the time, Thoreau stops short of calling for violent resistance. He still urges people only to resist the state by refusing to cooperate with it and refusing to accept its authority over them. But Thoreau became even more stringent in his abolitionist views after a shocking event in 1859: the raid on Harpers Ferry.

John Brown

John Brown first made a name for himself in Bleeding Kansas, where he led men in a number of battles and—more troublingly—in the Pottawatomie Massacre. He was well known for his actions, and President James Buchanan had even offered a $250 reward (nearly $7,000 in 2017) for his capture. In the abolitionist community, his means were controversial, but his dedication to the cause was beyond reproach. Among slave owners, his name often inspired fear due to his violent acts in Kansas.

Desiring to do more than free small numbers of slaves in Kansas, John Brown began formulating a much more ambitious plan. He wanted to instigate a slave rebellion across the South. He thought that if he could secure a large number of weapons, slaves would turn on their masters and flock to join him. Then, his army could wage a guerrilla war from the Appalachian Mountains, freeing slaves as they went.

Brown tried to recruit men for his daring attack on the South, but he struggled to do so. Many people doubted whether such a raid could succeed. However, many abolitionists did give him material support—money, guns, and lodging. At one point, Brown even met with Harriet Tubman. She helped him recruit African Americans to the cause, and some historians think she would have joined the raid herself had she not been ill at the time.

In the end, Brown could only find twenty-one people to accompany him: three of them were his own sons, and five of them were African American. He chose the arsenal at Harpers Ferry, Virginia, as the target of his attack. It contained one thousand firearms, enough to start a war if he could find people to wield them.

John Brown gained a reputation for humorlessness after his death, but contemporaries recalled he was fond of wordplay and never missed a joke.

On October 16, 1859, Brown put his plan into action. He marched on Harpers Ferry late at night and managed to seize the arsenal without firing a shot. However, the plan soon began to unravel as word of the attack spread. Brown took a number of hostages from the community, including the great-grandnephew of George Washington. He hoped this might discourage assaults on the arsenal, but it did not. Men in the local militia soon arrived, and a battle erupted. Citizens of the town were killed during the first day, along with some of Brown's men. Brown sent one of his sons and another man out under a white flag to negotiate for their escape in return for the hostages, but the militia shot them both.

The next day, Lieutenant Colonel Robert E. Lee arrived with a group of marines. (He would later gain fame as one of the South's most successful generals in the Civil War.) Lee attempted to negotiate for Brown's surrender, but Brown refused unless he and his men were released. Lee then ordered the arsenal stormed. His men pounded in the door with sledgehammers and rushed in with their bayonets fixed. They did not fire their weapons so as not to risk harming the hostages. One marine and two of Brown's men died in the fighting, but in the end, John Brown and the rest of his men were captured. Lee's description of the attack as "the attempt of a fanatic or madman" characterized the early public response to the incident.

Most of John Brown's men were killed in the two days of fighting or captured when the arsenal was stormed. Only a few escaped north with their lives. John Brown himself stood trial for his actions in Virginia. He was

A contemporaneous depiction of John Brown's men and hostages just before Lee's assault

convicted after a trial that barely lasted a week and was sentenced to die. Just one month later, he was hanged. Six of his men followed him to the gallows.

Brown was allowed to make a public statement after he was convicted. Completely unrepentant, he defended his actions and denounced slavery. However, he did say that he had hoped the raid would be less violent than it was—his chief aim was simply to help slaves escape to freedom.

One month later, on the way to his execution, Brown handed one of his guards a note with a chilling message: "I, John Brown, am now quite certain that the crimes of this guilty land can never be purged away but with blood. I had as I now think vainly flattered myself that without very much bloodshed it might be done." Just over a year later, the Civil War tore the nation in two.

John Brown's raid greatly increased tensions about slavery throughout the United States. Many African Americans and abolitionists publicly criticized his hasty execution. In turn, many Southerners suspected Northern abolitionists of greater involvement in the raid than they were willing to admit. Letters exchanged between John Brown and some prominent antislavery advocates were found and taken as proof of these suspicions, and many historians believe that John Brown's raid hastened the coming of the Civil War.

The legacy of John Brown as an individual is extremely controversial. Few are comfortable dismissing him as a madman, like Lee, or holding him up as a hero, like Thoreau. An uncompromising man, Brown was convinced of the evils of slavery and certain that his acts were just for that reason. However, it is easy to find fault with his violent methods—which often fell upon those who were by no means ardent supporters of slavery. In fact, the first person killed by Brown's party in Harpers Ferry was a freed African American who stood in their way. Brown's killing of five men at the Pottawatomie Massacre also bears remembering in any accounting of his life. The wife and mother of three of his Pottawatomie Massacre victims wrote the following letter to him while he awaited execution. It is a vivid reminder of the suffering that he caused in his crusade against slavery:

"

Altho' vengeance is not mine, I confess that I do feel gratified to hear that you were stopped in your fiendish career at Harpers Ferry, with the loss of your two sons, you can now appreciate my distress in Kansas, when you then and there entered my house at midnight and arrested my husband and two boys, and took them out of the yard and in cold blood shot them dead in my hearing. You can't say you done it to free slaves. We had none and never expected to own one.

A Plea for Captain John Brown

As news of John Brown's raid swept across the country, the initial reaction was to condemn Brown. Even abolitionist papers made it clear that they did not support his actions. One abolitionist paper, the *Liberator*, refers to Brown's raid as "a misguided, wild, and apparently insane—effort." It appeared as though Brown would find few friends in the North after his raid failed so spectacularly. However, Thoreau was not so quick to write off the fanatical abolitionist. He had met Brown one time before when Brown was touring New England in search of money to support his actions, although the two were no more than acquaintances.

In the month between Brown's conviction and execution, Thoreau composed a speech, "A Plea for Captain John Brown." He presented it a number of times at public gatherings in the short time frame before the execution. The speech is a strongly worded defense of the violent abolitionist. Thoreau lionizes Brown and builds him up as a larger-than-life figure. He also criticizes the Northern press for abandoning Brown, as well as anyone calling him insane or accusing him of throwing his life away. The following passage provides an example of the tone and content of the speech:

> *I wish I could say that Brown was the representative of the North. He was a superior man. He did not value his bodily life in comparison with ideal things. He did not recognize unjust human laws, but resisted them as he was bid. For once we are lifted out of the trivialness and dust of politics into the region of truth and manhood. No man in America has ever stood up so persistently and effectively for the dignity of human nature, knowing himself for a man, and the equal of any and all governments. In that sense he was the most American of us all. He needed no babbling lawyer, making false issues, to defend him. He was more than a match for all the judges that American voters, or office-holders of whatever grade, can create. He could not have been tried by a jury of his peers, because his peers did not exist.*

According to scholars, Thoreau's speech was an important turning point in the American view of John Brown. As time passed after the raid, Brown came to be seen more and more sympathetically. At first, Brown was abandoned by his fellow abolitionists, but after his death and Thoreau's speeches, they came to his defense in greater numbers.

Scholar George M. Shulam writes, "Thoreau's impassioned, incendiary speech initiated a decisive shift in northern public opinion, a shift that really registered in the South and encouraged southern support for secession. In a year the Civil War began." In this way, we can see just how important Thoreau's defense of Brown was to American history. After "A Plea for Captain John Brown," Thoreau would go on to write two more essays that defended Brown—this time after Brown's execution by the state of Virginia.

Thoreau and Nonviolence

Thoreau's defense of Brown raises a number of questions given the fact that Thoreau seemed committed to nonviolent resistance in his earlier political essay "Civil Disobedience." Scholars who study Thoreau have never fully resolved this apparent contradiction in Thoreau's writings. Some have argued that Thoreau himself never committed to the idea that only nonviolent resistance should be used. James J. Donahue writes, "Nowhere in any of Thoreau's political pieces is there any explicit prohibition of violence as a means to achieve an end, even if such is often read into his own nonviolent actions." In other words, Thoreau chose to use nonviolent protest, but he never condemned those who used violence to try to stop an injustice.

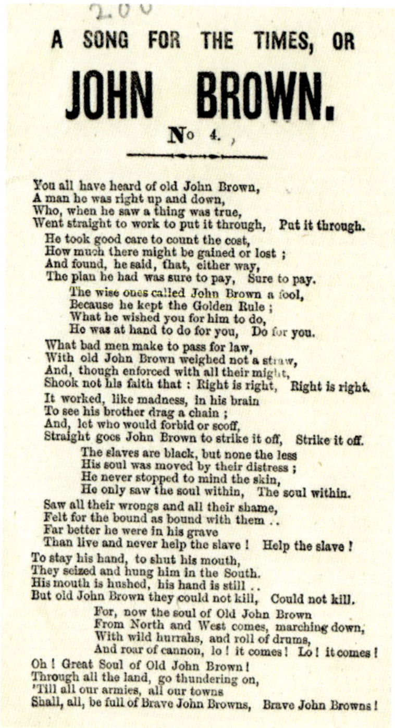

A SONG FOR THE TIMES, OR

JOHN BROWN.

No 4.

You all have heard of old John Brown,
A man he was right up and down,
Who, when he saw a thing was true,
Went straight to work to put it through, Put it through.

He took good care to count the cost,
How much there might be gained or lost;
And found, he said, that, either way,
The plan he had was sure to pay, Sure to pay.

The wise ones called John Brown a fool,
Because he kept the Golden Rule;
What he wished you for him to do,
He was at hand to do for you, Do for you.

What bad men make to pass for law,
With old John Brown weighed not a straw,
And, though enforced with all their might,
Shook not his faith that: Right is right, Right is right.

It worked, like madness, in his brain
To see his brother drag a chain;
And, let who would forbid or scoff,
Straight goes John Brown to strike it off, Strike it off.

The slaves are black, but none the less
His soul was moved by their distress;
He never stopped to mind the skin,
He only saw the soul within, The soul within.

Saw all their wrongs and all their shame,
Felt for the bound as bound with them ..
Far better he were in his grave
Than live and never help the slave! Help the slave!

To stay his hand, to shut his mouth,
They seized and hung him in the South.
His mouth is hushed, his hand is still ..
But old John Brown they could not kill, Could not kill.

For, now the soul of Old John Brown
From North and West comes, marching down,
With wild hurrahs, and roll of drums,
And roar of cannon, lo! it comes! Lo! it comes!

Oh! Great Soul of Old John Brown!
Through all the land, go thundering on,
'Till all our armies, all our towns
Shall, all, be full of Brave John Browns, Brave John Browns!

A song about John Brown was a popular Union marching song.

It is also possible that Thoreau's feelings on the subject changed over time. When he wrote "Civil Disobedience," the national debate over slavery was much more subdued than it was a decade later, in the aftermath of John Brown's raid. The Fugitive Slave Act and Dred Scott case had made abolitionists despair of any change occurring through peaceful means. It seemed the courts and legislature were united against them. This change in the national landscape may have occasioned a change in Thoreau's thoughts on the matter. Scholar Leon Edel points to this, writing that "Civil Disobedience" and Thoreau's later works concerning John Brown are "hardly the voice of the same man."

A third view is that Thoreau's political opinions are stable because they all focus on the individual and how the individual can challenge the state. Thoreau himself used nonviolent protest; later, Brown used violent rebellion. Both fit into the idea that it is up to upstanding individuals to resist a tyrannical state. Furthermore, some scholars argue that Thoreau saw Brown as a kind of transcendental hero for this reason. He was one freethinking individual who took it upon himself to take up the cause of justice. Donahue argues for this reading when he writes, "The John Brown pieces provide at first a focused defense of one particular man in whom Thoreau has identified the solution to slavery, followed by an abstract eulogy for a Transcendental hero."

It is not hard to see the merit of this view when you look at the text of "A Plea for Captain John Brown." More than just defend Brown, Thoreau tries to elevate him to mythical proportions. At one point, he writes:

> "
>
> *Some eighteen hundred years ago Christ was crucified; this morning, perchance, Captain Brown was hung. These are the two ends of a chain which is not without its links. He is not Old Brown any longer; he is an angel of light.*

Regardless of his motives, Thoreau's writings on John Brown present a contrast to his much more famous work "Civil Disobedience." The essays and speeches on John Brown would be the last political works he published. He died just two and a half years after Brown, at home in Concord, while the Civil War raged to the south.

Frederick Douglass

While history books often focus on white abolitionists such as Thoreau and John Brown, African American abolitionists were just as important to the movement, if not more important. Perhaps the best-known African American abolitionist is Frederick Douglass, who was himself an escaped slave. Douglass was born to a mother who was a slave in Maryland in 1818. The identity of his father is not known, although Douglass reported many thought it was the white man who owned his mother. He spent his early years toiling on plantations in Maryland before working in a shipyard in Baltimore. Finally, he was able to escape to the North from Baltimore when he was approximately twenty years old (he did not know his own birthday since such records were often lacking for slaves).

Once he was free, Douglass became an ardent campaigner for the end of slavery. He published his own story of life in bondage, *Narrative of the Life of Frederick Douglass, an American Slave*. It became one of the most widely read slave narratives of the time and advanced the abolitionist cause. He toured not only the United States (in the North) but Ireland and Britain as well, speaking out against the evils of slavery.

In 1847, Douglass met John Brown for the first time. He was impressed with the radical abolitionist, who told Douglass of his plans to fight slavery with arms, and Brown later stayed in Douglass's home for a month while planning his attack. Just before the ill-fated raid on Harpers Ferry, Douglass met with Brown one final time in a stone quarry. A fugitive slave by the name of Shield Green accompanied him. Brown tried to convince Douglass to join the assault himself and for the first time told Douglass of the target: the federal arsenal. Douglass was horrified. Convinced that his plan would fail, he tried to dissuade Brown, but Brown would not be swayed. Douglass refused to join him, though Brown did convince Green to join the assault. Green was hanged after the raid. After the failed raid, Douglass fled to Canada as news of his connection to Brown became public.

Like Thoreau, Douglass lionized John Brown in the years to come—even though he thought his mission foolhardy when it was planned. After the end of the Civil War and emancipation of the slaves, Douglass continued to campaign for social progress. After African American men were granted the right to vote, he was a vocal advocate for women's suffrage—extending the right to vote to women.

Douglass died in 1895 at the age of seventy-seven. He had witnessed and effected great changes in the plight of African Americans during his long life. Born into slavery, he saw the evil institution end. Today, he is remembered as one of the most important African Americans of his day. His tireless campaigning for justice and civil rights for all inspired his contemporaries and still serves as a reminder of how great an impact one man can make on the lives of so many others.

Martin Luther King Jr. delivers his "I Have a Dream" speech in Washington, DC.

CHAPTER FOUR

The Effects of Civil Disobedience

After the end of slavery and the death of Thoreau, "Civil Disobedience" might have faded away. It was not given much attention even during his own life, and his later political writings were chiefly about abolitionism: a topic of little relevance after the Civil War. To make matters worse, Thoreau's literary executor began stripping all of his political works from books published in Thoreau's name. Rather than market books about radical political views, he hoped to promote Thoreau as a great American nature writer.

It was in England that Thoreau's political works were saved from obscurity. His night in jail, which many

Americans did not take too seriously, was respected more in England. A social reformer by the name of Henry Stephens Salt published a biography of Thoreau in 1890, and this helped bring Thoreau's political works to a wider audience. Salt was active not just in the field of literary criticism but also in organizations promoting vegetarianism, prison reform, and pacifism. It is through Salt and his interest in social causes that Thoreau's works reached both Mahatma Gandhi and Leo Tolstoy—the world-renowned Russian writer.

These connections ensured that Thoreau's "Civil Disobedience" would never be forgotten. Tolstoy and Gandhi—towering figures in modern history—referred often to their respect for Thoreau and his short piece "Civil Disobedience." As a result, Martin Luther King Jr. later encountered the essay and was greatly inspired by it. Although largely neglected during Thoreau's own lifetime, "Civil Disobedience" is now widely respected as an important step in the history of nonviolent protest and American protest in general.

Leo Tolstoy

Tolstoy was born in Russia in 1828, just eleven years after Henry David Thoreau. But he lived until the age of ninety-two, well into the twentieth century, unlike Thoreau, who died quite young. As a result, Tolstoy's works that mention

Count Leo Tolstoy

Thoreau often seem to belong to a different era, rather than to a man just eleven years his junior.

Tolstoy was a member of the Russian aristocracy, but his formative years were difficult. Both of his parents died young, as well as his next guardian, an aunt. He was educated at his family's estate by tutors until he entered university. However, his university career proved difficult, and he dropped out three years later without graduating. His life then entered a dark period. He described it many years later in his work *A Confession*:

> *I cannot think of those years without horror, loathing and heartache. I killed men in war and challenged men to duels in order to kill them. I lost at cards, consumed the labor of the peasants, sentenced them to punishments, lived loosely, and deceived people. Lying, robbery, adultery of all kinds, drunkenness, violence, murder—there was no crime I did not commit, and in spite of that people praised my conduct and my contemporaries considered and consider me to be a comparatively moral man.*

In 1851, Tolstoy joined the army in an attempt to live a more structured life and overcome his vices. He served during a number of military campaigns, yet even at this time his writings seem to hint at his later pacifist beliefs. He published his first works during this period, but many of his stories were heavily censored by the Russian press because they were less than sympathetic toward the war.

After leaving the army, Tolstoy traveled around Europe for a number of years. In 1857, Tolstoy visited Paris. What was supposed to be pleasant trip soon took on a much more serious tone. Tolstoy went to view a public execution by guillotine, and he was horrified by what he saw. A healthy man one instant was dead a split second later because of a judge's decree. Throughout his life, he looked back to that day many times: it was a shocking, vivid image of just how violent the state could be.

Tolstoy returned to his estate in Russia and opened a school for peasants in 1861. This was a progressive step at the time. It was the same year that serfs in Russia were finally granted their freedom. While serfs before this were not technically slaves because the noble in control of their lives did not own them, they had few freedoms. They were unable to travel from their estate or even marry without the consent of the noble whose land they lived on. Tolstoy's school was his first attempt at social reform and humanitarian work. His acts did not go unnoticed by the oppressive Russian state, and his school and family

Tolstoy took part in fierce fighting in the Caucasus Mountains, depicted here, during his time in the army.

estate were raided by the secret police. Tolstoy shut down the school for the time being.

Around the same time, Tolstoy met and married his wife, Sophia Andreyevna Behrs, over a matter of months. Their relationship was important for the rest of Tolstoy's life—she outlived him, and they had thirteen children together. Their early years of marriage were quite happy. Over the next fifteen years, Tolstoy wrote and published *War and Peace* and *Anna Karenina*—his two most famous masterpieces. Today, they are regarded as two of the most important novels ever written, and they secured Tolstoy's legacy as one of the most influential writers in human history.

The Tolstoyan Movement

In later years, Tolstoy grappled with periods of intense depression. His depression only lifted after he had a spiritual awakening that shaped the later years of his life. Tolstoy became a devout Christian who looked to the gospels for inspirations, rather than to any organized religion. As a result, his views were extreme by many people's standards. He was a devoted pacifist, and he completely rejected the state as illegitimate due to its reliance on violence. Furthermore, large numbers of followers subscribed to Tolstoy's religious and political philosophy and called themselves Tolstoyans. Tolstoy himself advocated for civil disobedience, and it was during this later period of his life that he came to embrace the works of Thoreau.

Tolstoy makes a number of passing references to Thoreau in his writings. He is always complimentary and seems to see much of his own views reflected in the American author who lived a generation before him. One of the longest references to Thoreau in Tolstoy's writings is found in his published "Letter to Dr. Schmitt":

> "
>
> *You write to me that people seem quite unable to understand that to serve the government is incompatible with Christianity.*

> *In just the same way people were long unable to see that indulgences, inquisitions, slavery, and tortures were incompatible with Christianity. But a time came when it was comprehensible; and a time will come when men will understand the incompatibility with Christianity, first of war service (that already is beginning to be felt), and then of service to government in general.*
>
> *It is now fifty years since a not widely known, but very remarkable, American writer Thoreau not only clearly expressed that incompatibility in his admirable essay on "Civil Disobedience," but gave a practical example of such disobedience. Not wishing to be an accomplice or supporter of a government which legalized slavery, he declined to pay a tax demanded of him, and went to prison for it.*

Later scholars have pointed out that Tolstoy seems to misrepresent Thoreau here, to a small degree. While Tolstoy ascribes his nonviolent resistance to Christian morals, Thoreau himself said it was a matter of conscience and did not focus on any religious arguments.

But Thoreau's influence is perhaps most important in a letter that does not mention him by name: "A Letter to a Hindu." In it, Tolstoy urges the people of India to resist

Tolstoyans flocked to Tolstoy's manor in the Russian countryside to meet the Russian intellectual.

the British Empire, which controlled their land, through nonviolent means:

> *The law of love, which excludes all resistance by violence, is natural to men's hearts and is even now revealed to them. As soon as men live entirely in accord with this law and hold aloof from all participation in violence, not only will hundreds be unable to enslave millions, but not even millions will be able to enslave a single individual. Do not resist the evil-doer and take no part in doing so, either in the violent deeds of the administration, in the law courts, in the collection of taxes, or above all in soldiering, and no one in the world will be able to enslave you.*

The letter, penned in 1908, shaped the life of an Indian man who read it—Mohandas Gandhi. Gandhi wrote to Tolstoy after reading it to seek permission to translate it into Gujarati and distribute it across India. Tolstoy was happy to oblige, and the two men corresponded until Tolstoy's death—the last letter that Tolstoy wrote was to Gandhi.

Mohandas Gandhi

Mohandas Gandhi (later called Mahatma) was born in Gujarat, India, in 1869. He came from a wealthy family and went to London to become a lawyer. He spent three years there before returning to India a barrister. Through a shared interest in vegetarianism, he came upon the works of Henry Salt—and his writings about Henry David Thoreau. The ideas he read in "Civil Disobedience" influenced his later actions and beliefs as the leader of India's independence movement.

He moved to South Africa—at the time controlled by the British Empire, like India—in 1893 to practice law. South Africa was a strictly segregated society with blacks, whites, and Indians subject to different laws due to their race. The deeply racist system oppressed blacks and Indians, and Gandhi experienced this firsthand. One day, when he was riding in a first-class train car, he was asked to move because a white passenger complained about his

Gandhi in his later years

being there. Armed with his ticket, Gandhi refused. He was physically removed from the train. It was his first act of civil disobedience, but not his last.

Gandhi spent the next twenty-one years fighting for greater rights for Indians in South Africa. He founded the Natal Indian Congress to accomplish this goal and headed the organization. It was during this time that Gandhi first used his strategy of Satyagraha. Gandhi explains the Sanskrit word in the following way:

> *Truth (satya) implies love, and firmness (agraha) engenders and therefore serves as a synonym for force. I thus began to call the Indian movement Satyagraha, that is to say, the Force which is born of Truth and Love or non-violence, and gave up the use of the phrase "passive resistance" in connection with it, so much so that even in English writing we often avoided it and used instead the word "satyagraha" itself or some other equivalent English phrase.*

In practice, Satyagraha meant that Gandhi encouraged tens of thousands of Indians to disobey discriminatory laws in South Africa. Many went to jail, including Gandhi, but eventually the government relented and did away with many of the oppressive laws. It was a defining period in Gandhi's life, where he utilized many of the techniques he would soon put to use in India.

The exact nature of Thoreau's influence on Gandhi's Satyagraha movement is complex. Gandhi himself rejected the idea that "Civil Disobedience" was directly responsible for his movement. In a letter, he wrote:

> *The resistance to authority in South Africa was well advanced before I got the essay of Thoreau on civil disobedience. But the movement was then known as passive resistance. As it was incomplete I had coined the word satyagraha for the Gujarati readers. When I saw the title of Thoreau's great essay, I began the use of his phrase to explain our struggle to the English readers. But I found that even civil disobedience failed to convey the full meaning of the struggle. I therefore adopted the phrase civil resistance. Non-violence was always an integral part of our struggle.*

It is clear that Gandhi respected Thoreau, but in his letter he does not credit Thoreau with a great influence on his campaign. Instead, he mostly gives Thoreau credit for the phrase "civil disobedience," which he used only briefly to translate "Satyagraha" into English.

However, it is interesting to note that Gandhi used Thoreau's essay "Civil Disobedience" to justify his campaign of Satyagraha in its early days. In 1907, he published a translation of the essay in a newspaper, with an introduction that includes the claim, "Historians say that the chief cause of the abolition of slavery in America was Thoreau's imprisonment and the publication by him of the above-mentioned book after his release." It was a bold claim, one that Gandhi undoubtedly knew was false as a matter of history. But it did serve to defend the idea that civil disobedience could lead to widespread social change by appealing to a fictionalized version of American history and Thoreau's importance during his own lifetime.

Indian Independence

Gandhi returned to India in 1915. There he played a major role in the Indian struggle for independence from Great Britain. In 1919, British India passed the Rowlatt Acts, which allowed the government to imprison people without trial and crack down on dissent. The effort to stop the movement for Indian independence failed. Gandhi launched a major Satyagraha campaign to oppose the measure and urged people across India to engage in civil disobedience. Students dropped out of school, government officials resigned, and citizens refused to pay taxes. Gandhi was arrested and sent to prison, but the desire for an independent India could not be stopped so easily.

After being released from prison two years later, Gandhi initially turned his attention to matters other than independence. He tried to bring Indian political parties together and launched various social campaigns to improve the lives of Indians. However, in 1930 he led the Salt March, one of the most famous acts of civil disobedience in history. The British had banned the collection of salt from the sea so that they could have a monopoly on its production. Indians were forced to buy salt from the government, and this was a source of revenue for the British Empire. Gandhi marched with a group of supporters some 240 miles (386 km) from an inland city to the coast of India, declaring his intent to ignore the law and collect salt once he arrived. He spoke to thousands of Indians in villages along the way, and the press covered his march extensively. When he reached the sea, he picked up a lump of natural salt from the coast and urged Indians all along the coast to do the same. They listened, and more than sixty thousand Indians were arrested for the illegal production of salt.

Gandhi continued agitating for independence. His dream became a reality in 1947 when India and Pakistan became independent nations and were no longer part of the British Empire. However, six months later Gandhi was assassinated by an Indian extremist who thought he was too sympathetic toward the government of Pakistan—the conflict between the Hindu-majority nation of India and the Muslim-majority nation of Pakistan was already tearing the region apart.

Nevertheless, Gandhi's campaign of Satyagraha remained a powerful example of what nonviolent civil disobedience could accomplish. It had defeated the British Empire peacefully and won self-determination for millions of people in India and Pakistan.

Martin Luther King Jr.

Thoreau is often considered the first major figure in America's rich tradition of civil disobedience, but the most important figure is likely Martin Luther King Jr. Born in Atlanta, Georgia, in 1929, King grew up in the rigid system of racial segregation of the American South. Discrimination was a daily fact of life at the time, and public services such as schools and buses were segregated according to the color of one's skin.

King excelled in school and skipped two grades. As a result, he entered Morehead College at the young age of fifteen. It was there that he first read "Civil Disobedience."

Later, he wrote the following about the importance of that fact to this life:

> *During my student days I read Henry David Thoreau's essay "On Civil Disobedience" for the first time. Here, in the courageous New Englander's refusal to pay his taxes and his choice of jail rather than support a war that would spread slavery's territory into Mexico, I made my first contact with the theory of non-violent resistance. Fascinated by the idea of refusing to cooperate with an evil system, I was so deeply moved that I reread the work several times.*

Unlike Gandhi, King always credited Thoreau as a major inspiration for his later protests, and he referred to Thoreau's work repeatedly.

Civil Rights Movement

After graduating from college, King went to seminary before going on to Boston University and receiving his PhD. He became a pastor in 1954, and his Christian faith played a large role in his public and private life. In 1955, King became a nationally renowned civil rights leader with the Montgomery bus boycott. The boycott was inspired

Rosa Parks worked as a seamstress before becoming a civil rights leader.

by the arrest of Rosa Parks for refusing to give up her seat to a white passenger on a city bus. King urged the entire African American community to stop riding the bus to protest her arrest and the segregation of black and white passengers. For more than a year, African Americans—formerly more than half the passengers—stopped riding the city buses. The boycott only stopped when a court found the segregated bus system unconstitutional, bringing an end to the issue. After the boycott, King remained the civil rights leader with the highest national profile, and he continued to fight for equal rights for African Americans.

At the time, the **civil rights movement** was confronting discrimination and segregation throughout the country. It was a diverse movement, with some advocating violence and a withdrawal from white society while others advocated nonviolent protest and further integration as equals. King was not the leader of the entire movement—he was only one of many. His major position after the Montgomery bus boycott was as president of the Southern Christian Leadership Conference (SCLC). It was in this capacity that he led the Birmingham campaign of 1963.

Birmingham, Alabama, was one of the most segregated cities at the time, with a long history of police brutality and unfair court decisions against African Americans. King led a series of nonviolent protests seeking to change the system of segregation and oppression. Protesters marched and demonstrated without permission from the city. They engaged in sit-ins, shutting down segregated businesses until they were arrested. The Birmingham jail eventually filled with protesters, but the demonstrations continued. The Birmingham police responded with violence.

Demonstrators are sprayed by fire hoses as they protest segregation in Birmingham, Alabama.

High-pressure fire hoses and police dogs were turned on protesters, including children and students. The images and video of the events shocked the United States and the world.

King was arrested in the course of the protest. From his cell, he wrote "Letter from Birmingham Jail," one of the most important pieces of literature from the civil rights movement and an impassioned defense of nonviolent resistance against oppression. He defends the Birmingham campaign from critics who argued that negotiation, rather than protest, should have been used:

> *You may well ask: "Why direct action? Why sit ins, marches and so forth? Isn't negotiation a better path?" You are quite right in calling for negotiation. Indeed, this is the very purpose of direct action. Nonviolent direct action seeks to create such a crisis and foster such a tension that a community which has constantly refused to negotiate is forced to confront the issue. It seeks so to dramatize the issue that it can no longer be ignored. My citing the creation of tension as part of the work of the nonviolent resister may sound rather shocking. But I must confess that I am not afraid of the word "tension." I have earnestly opposed violent tension, but there is a*

> *type of constructive, nonviolent tension which is necessary for growth … The purpose of our direct action program is to create a situation so crisis packed that it will inevitably open the door to negotiation. I therefore concur with you in your call for negotiation. Too long has our beloved Southland been bogged down in a tragic effort to live in monologue rather than dialogue.*

The same year, King took part in the March on Washington for Jobs and Freedom. He delivered his famous "I Have a Dream" speech from the steps of the Lincoln Memorial. It was a powerful call for an end to racism and discrimination that reverberated around the world.

King's leadership in the civil rights movement continued until 1968—the year that is generally considered the movement's end. With the passage of a number of laws, the voting rights and housing opportunities of African Americans were finally protected to a large degree. However, King did not retire from public life. He continued to fight injustice, becoming an outspoken critic of the Vietnam War.

On April 4, 1968, Martin Luther King Jr. was assassinated, but his accomplishments live on. During his life, he was honored with many awards and medals—including the Nobel Peace Prize in 1964. Since his death, countless buildings, streets, and other sites have been

Thoreau's Cultural Influence

Thoreau has remained relevant to current events long after his death in 1862. Artists and reformers have turned to many of his works for inspiration and adapted ideas that he first put forward to suit their own times.

In 1970, two playwrights by the name of Jerome Lawrence and Robert E. Lee wrote *The Night Thoreau Spent in Jail*. The work portrays various scenes from Thoreau's life, including the death of his brother, his short-lived romance with a woman whom his brother proposed to first, and his time in jail in Concord. The play centers on Thoreau's life, but its real topic was just as much the ongoing and deeply unpopular Vietnam War of the time. Thoreau's denunciation of a corrupt government engaging in an immoral war was not meant to be only a matter of history. In this way, Thoreau's message was presented in a way that was relevant to the times.

A *New York Times* review of the play by Howard Taubman explains just how relevant the play was at the time:

> *Whatever its merits as a work of art, this play and its protagonist, though they are of the nineteenth century, are speaking to today's concerns: an unwanted war in another land, civil disobedience, the interdependence of man and nature, education, the role of government and the governed. And audiences are responding as if Thoreau were their contemporary, which in the large sense he is.*

Thoreau's work *Walden* has also inspired a number of works in response to it. The influential psychologist B. F. Skinner wrote a utopian novel titled *Walden Two* that was published in 1948. It focuses on a community of people who live in a fictional utopia in the modern world. All their problems are solved through behavior modification, and the community members live happy, fulfilling lives. In the novel, Skinner explores the idea of self-reliance in a community, rather than on an individual level as Thoreau did in *Walden*.

It has been a controversial work, but one that has also inspired real-world events. In 1969, an **intentional community**, Twin Oaks Community, was started in Virginia based on many of the ideas contained in *Walden Two*. While it has since distanced itself from some of the ideas presented in *Walden Two*, it still exists and uses many of the practical organization tools that appear in *Walden Two*. For example, members are expected to earn a certain number of labor credits (hours of work) a week to contribute to the community.

Twin Oaks Community currently has more than one hundred members who live and work together in rural Virginia. They support themselves through various business enterprises, such as hammock making and tofu production, as well as raising livestock. Most of their property is communal and shared by all members. For example, no member personally owns a car at the community. Instead, they all share seventeen vehicles. In the lives of the people at the community, the words of Thoreau can still be seen to have an impact even today, more than a century and a half after his death.

named after him both in the United States and abroad. His commitment to human rights and justice has inspired people around the world.

A Lasting Legacy

Thoreau lived just forty-four years, but he accomplished an extraordinary amount in that time. His passion was always nature, and it is fitting that his book *Walden*, about living a simple life surrounded by nature, is his most well-known work. Read in high schools across the country, it is, in the words of John Updike, “a totem of the back-to-nature, preservationist, anti-business, civil-disobedience mindset.” The book inspires many people who champion different causes; they all see their concerns reflected in the inspiring words of Thoreau. *Walden* was an important predecessor of the modern environmentalist movement, and to this day it is cited as a testament to the importance of nature.

But it is not Thoreau’s love of nature that had the greatest effect on history. It was his refusal to sit silently by and pretend not to see the horrors of slavery and war that gripped the United States of his day. Thoreau—a man with no political ambitions—found himself forced to enter the political arena and take a stand on the side of justice and human dignity. His refusal to pay taxes, no doubt viewed as a bizarre act by his neighbors in Concord, was necessary according to his conscience.

Sitting in a Concord jail cell, Thoreau could not have imagined the lasting impact his one night in jail would have on the world. Although he was not the first to protest war and slavery by refusing to pay taxes, his persuasive defense of his actions in "Civil Disobedience" changed human history. Generally ignored by his contemporaries, the essay would later inspire Tolstoy, Gandhi, and King, as well as countless others, to practice nonviolent resistance and civil disobedience.

Its appeal to withdraw one's allegiance from a corrupt government resonated with people around the world in many different eras. Thoreau's ideas would later be borrowed by diverse movements such as anarchism and libertarianism as a defense of the idea that government should be as small as possible, or even nonexistent. Its celebration of the individual—and his or her potential—inspired countless people to confront injustice in their daily lives and be silent witnesses no longer.

There is no question that "Civil Disobedience" has shaped the history of the modern world. The nonviolent movements of both Gandhi and King might have been very different without the eloquent essay by Thoreau. In turn, the successes of Gandhi and King's movements served as important examples of the power of nonviolent protest. Many other social and political reform movements that might very well have been violent have instead been inspired to seek change through peaceful means.

CHRONOLOGY

1817	David Henry Thoreau (who later reverses his first and middle names) is born in Concord, Massachusetts.
1835	The Texas Revolution begins in Mexico.
1837	Thoreau graduates from Harvard and takes a short-lived job as a teacher.
1846	The Mexican-American War begins; Thoreau is thrown in jail for a night after refusing to pay his poll tax.
1848	The Treaty of Guadalupe Hidalgo ends the Mexican-American War .
1849	Thoreau publishes "Civil Disobedience" (then titled "Resistance to Civil Government").
1850	The Compromise of 1850, including the Fugitive Slave Act, is passed by Congress. Abolitionists are outraged.
1854	Thoreau publishes *Walden*, his most famous book.
1857	The Dred Scott case is decided, and the rights of citizens are taken away from African Americans throughout the United States.
1859	John Brown is executed after his failed raid at Harpers Ferry. Thoreau publishes the first of three essays in Brown's defense.

1861 The American Civil War begins.

1862 Thoreau dies in Concord.

1865 The American Civil War ends, and slavery is abolished across the United States.

1930 Gandhi leads the Salt March and inspires millions to practice civil disobedience by making their own salt unlawfully.

1947 Gandhi's struggle for an independent India comes to an end when Great Britain recognizes it and Pakistan as independent states.

1963 Martin Luther King Jr. delivers the "I Have a Dream" speech in Washington, DC.

1970 *The Night Thoreau Spent in Jail* premieres on stages across the United States.

GLOSSARY

abolitionist Someone who campaigns for the end of slavery.

anarchist Someone who supports the political philosophy of anarchism—the idea that people should not be governed by a state.

civil disobedience The refusal to abide by certain laws of a state. It often takes the form of nonviolent resistance, such as tax resistance and sit-ins.

civil rights movement The movement to end racial segregation and discrimination in the United States between the years of 1954 and 1968.

Dred Scott case The US Supreme Court ruling that African Americans, whether enslaved or free, do not possess the rights of citizens. The 1857 decision is widely regarded as one of the worst in the court's history.

Fugitive Slave Act Part of the Compromise of 1850, the act made it easier for masters to have escaped slaves returned to them from the North. It outraged abolitionists.

intentional community A community of people who often share resources among their members and live an alternative lifestyle different from wider society in some way.

Kansas-Nebraska Act A law passed in 1854 that allowed the new states of Kansas and Nebraska to determine for themselves whether to be slave states or Free States.

manifest destiny The belief that the United States was destined to expand westward to the Pacific Ocean.

Missouri Compromise The compromise in 1820 that saw Maine admitted as a Free State and Missouri as a slave state. It also tried to settle the issue of slavery's expansion in the West by outlawing it in states created above the 36°30′ parallel (except for Missouri); however, this was later overturned with the Kansas-Nebraska Act of 1854.

nonviolent resistance Peaceful resistance toward a government with the aim of social change. Common methods of nonviolent resistance include protests, boycotts, and strikes.

popular sovereignty Most broadly, the idea that the government is created by the people and should rule insofar as it respects their wishes. In this context, it refers to the idea that states (and their people) should be able to settle the issue of slavery individually.

posse comitatus Men from the community who help law enforcement, often by apprehending a wanted man. Today, the word "posse" alone is often used–for instance, in Westerns.

Pottawatomie Massacre The murder of five people in Kansas by John Brown and men he led. The victims were believed to be supporters of slavery.

powder-monkeys Young boys in the navies of the era who were responsible for bringing gunpowder to the ship's cannons from its storage area (far from the scene of the fight).

prig A self-righteous person; the word often implies the person feels superior toward others.

Quakers Members of a Christian group that immigrated to the United States in large numbers to escape persecution in Europe. Quakers are pacifists, and for this reason they have a long history of civil disobedience to avoid supporting the government in times of war.

Treaty of Guadalupe Hidalgo The treaty signed in 1848 that ended the Mexican-American War.

Walden Thoreau's book published in 1854 that describes his life at a cabin beside Walden Pond.

Wilmot Proviso An attempt to ban slavery in any territory gained from the Mexican-American War. It was defeated by Southern congressmen.

FURTHER INFORMATION

Books

Cramer, Jeffrey S., ed. *The Quotable Thoreau*. Princeton, NJ: Princeton University Press, 2011.

Halpin, Mikki. *It's Your World–If You Don't Like It, Change It: Activism for Teenagers*. New York: Simon Pulse, 2008.

Harding, Walter. *The Days of Henry Thoreau*. Mineola, NY: Dover Publications, 2013.

Thoreau, Henry David. *Civil Disobedience and Other Essays*. Mineola, NY: Dover Publications, 1993.

Videos

"Henry David Thoreau's Civil Disobedience"

http://www.history.com/topics/homestead-strike/videos/henry-david-thoreaus-civil-disobedience

Actor David Strathairn reads an excerpt of "Civil Disobedience" after an introduction by Danny Glover.

"Thoreau and Civil Disobedience"

https://www.youtube.com/watch?v=gugnXTN6-D4

The School of Life describes Thoreau's night in jail and his political views in this video.

Websites

Civil Disobedience and Our Radical Moment

http://www.thoreausociety.org/news-article/wen-stephenson-civil-disobedience-and-our-radical-moment

The Thoreau Society presents a blog post by Wen Stephenson that examines the links between Thoreau and modern-day political protesters.

Hard Road to Texas: Texas Annexation 1836–1845

https://www.tsl.texas.gov/exhibits/annexation/index.html

The Texas State Library and Archives details the annexation of Texas—a process that would lead to the Mexican-American War.

Henry David Thoreau's Civil Disobedience

https://www.libertarianism.org/guides/lectures/henry-david-thoreaus-civil-disobedience

This lecture discusses Thoreau and his essay "Civil Disobedience" and features questions to consider while listening.

A History of Slavery in the United States

http://www.nationalgeographic.org/interactive/slavery-united-states

National Geographic provides a detailed timeline of slavery in the United States.

BIBLIOGRAPHY

Blight, David W. "Admiration and Ambivalence: Frederick Douglass and John Brown." The Gilder Lehrman Institute of American History. Retrieved March 1, 2017. https://www.gilderlehrman.org/history-by-era/failure-compromise/essays/admiration-and-ambivalence-frederick-douglass-and-john-brow.

Chernus, Ira. *American Nonviolence: The History of an Idea.* Maryknoll, NY: Orbis Books, 2013.

Donahue, James J. "'Hardly the Voice of the Same Man': 'Civil Disobedience' and Thoreau's Response to John Brown." *Midwest Quarterly* 48, no. 2 (Winter 2007): 247–265.

Douglass, Frederick. *Narrative of the Life of Frederick Douglass.* Ballingslöv, Sweden: Winehouse Classics, 2015.

Emerson, Ralph Waldo. "Thoreau." *Atlantic,* August 1862. https://www.theatlantic.com/magazine/archive/1862/08/thoreau/306418.

Fiala, Andrew. "Political Skepticism and Anarchist Themes in the American Tradition." *European Journal of Pragmatism and American Philosophy* 5, no. 2 (2013): 90–104.

Finkelman, Paul. "The Abolition of the Slave Trade." New York Public Library: Schomburg Center for Research in Black Culture. Retrieved March 1, 2017. http://abolition.nypl.org/essays/us_constitution/3.

Greenberg, Amy S. *A Wicked War: Polk, Clay, Lincoln, and the 1846 U.S. Invasion of Mexico*. New York: Vintage, 2012.

Hardiman, David. "Towards a History of Non-violent Resistance." *Economic and Political Weekly* 48, no. 23 (June 8, 2013): 41–48.

Horton, James Oliver, and Lois E. Horton. *Slavery and the Making of America*. Oxford, UK: Oxford University Press, 2004.

Jayne, Allen. *Jefferson's Declaration of Independence: Origins, Philosophy, and Theology*. Lexington: University Press of Kentucky, 2000.

Menchaca, Martha. *Recovering History, Constructing Race: The Indian, Black, and White Roots of Mexican Americans*. Austin: University of Texas Press, 2002.

Merry, Robert W. *A Country of Vast Designs: James K. Polk, the Mexican War, and the Conquest of the American Continent*. New York: Simon & Schuster, 2009.

Myerson, Joel, Sandra Harbert Petrulionis, and Laura Dassow Walls, eds. *The Oxford Handbook of Transcendentalism*. Oxford, UK: Oxford University Press, 2010.

Newman, Lance. "Thoreau and Violence." *Concord Saunterer* 23 (2015): 110–114.

Oates, Stephen B. *To Purge This Land with Blood: A Biography of John Brown*. Amherst: University of Massachusetts Press, 1984.

Petrulionis, Sandra Harbert, ed. *Thoreau in His Own Time: A Biographical Chronicle of His Life, Drawn From Recollections, Interviews, and Memoirs by Family, Friends, and Associates.* Iowa City: University of Iowa Press, 2012.

Schulman, George. *American Prophecy: Race and Redemption in American Political Culture*. Minneapolis: University of Minnesota Press, 2008.

Stevenson, Robert Louis. "Henry David Thoreau: His Character and Opinions." *Cornhill Magazine*, June 1880.

Taubman, Howard. "On Stage, Thoreau Speaks to Today." *New York Times*, December 23, 1970. http://www.nytimes.com/1970/12/23/archives/on-stage-thoreau-speaks-to-today.html.

Taylor, Bob Pepperman. *The Routledge Guidebook to Thoreau's Civil Disobedience.* Abingdon, UK: Routledge, 2014.

Thoreau, Henry David. *Civil Disobedience and Other Essays.* Mineola, NY: Dover Publications, 1993.

Thoreau, Henry David. *Walden; or, Life in the Woods*. Mineola, NY: Dover Publications, 1995.

Updike, John. "A Sage for All Seasons." *Guardian*, June 25, 2004. https://www.theguardian.com/books/2004/jun/26/classics.

Watts, Dale E. "How Bloody Was Bleeding Kansas?: Political Killings in Kansas Territory, 1854–1861." *Kansas History: A Journal of the Central Plains* 18, no. 2 (Summer 1995): 116–129.

INDEX

Page numbers in **boldface** are illustrations. Entries in **boldface** are glossary terms.

abolitionist, 8, 17, 27, 29, 31, 45, 48, 50, 54, 59, 61–62, 65, 67–68, 70, 72
anarchist, 55, 97

Birmingham campaign, 91–93, **91**
Bleeding Kansas, 29, 61–62, 66–67
Brown, John, 29, 61–73, **63**, **64**
Burns, Anthony, 59–60

Calhoun, John C., 42
"Civil Disobedience," 7, 17, 50–59, **50**, 69–71, 75–76, 81, 83, 85–86, 88–89, 97
civil rights movement, 5–7, 48, 58 **74**, 89–93, **91**, 97
Civil War, 7, 20, 29, 31, 64–65, 69, 71, 73, 75
Compromise of 1850, 41, 43–45, 59–61, 70
Constitution, 23–24, 38, 44, 61

Declaration of Independence, 21–23
Douglass, Frederick, 72–73
Dred Scott case, 30–31, 70

Emerson, Ralph Waldo, 10–13, **11**, 15–16, 50

Fugitive Slave Act, 43–45, 59–61, 70

Gandhi, Mahatma, 5–7, 48–49, 58, 76, 83–89, **84**, 97
Giddings, Joshua, 38–39

Harpers Ferry raid, 61–73, **64**

individualism, 11, 47, 56–59, 61, 70–71, 95, 97
intentional community, 95

Kansas-Nebraska Act, 27–29, 41, 43, 60

King, Martin Luther, Jr., 5–7, 48, 58, **74**, 76, 88–92, 96–97

Lee, Robert E., 63–64, **64**, 66
"Letter from Birmingham Jail," 92–93
Lincoln, Abraham, 37–38

manifest destiny, 35
March on Washington for Jobs and Freedom, **74**, 93
Mexican-American War
  aftermath of, 40–41, **40**
  background of, 31–36
  events of, 36–37, 39–40
  opposition to, 6–7, 19, 31, 37–39, 42, 51–54, 89, 96–97
Missouri Compromise, 27–29, 41
Montgomery bus boycott, 89–91

Night Thoreau Spent in Jail, The, 94

pacifism, 54, 76, 78, 80
Parks, Rosa, 89–90, **90**
"Plea for Captain John Brown, A," 67–71
Polk, James, 34–38, **35**, 41
popular sovereignty, 27–29, 43
posse comitatus, 57
Pottawatomie Massacre, 29, 61–62, 66–67
powder-monkeys, 56
prig, 16

Quakers, 54

Salt, Henry Stephens, 76, 83
Salt March, 87
Santa Anna, Antonio López de, 33–34, 39
Satyagraha, 84–88
slavery
  history of, **18**, 20–21, 25–26, **26**
  laws about, 23–24, 27–31, 41, 43–45, 59–61, 70
  opposition to, 6–8, 17, 19–20, 22–23, 26, 45, 48, 50–

54, 58–62, 70, 72–73, 81, 86, 89, 96–97
support of, 42
Texas and, 33–34, 42–43
violent conflict over, 7, 20, 29, 31, 59, 61–67, **64**, 71, 73
"Slavery in Massachusetts," 59–61

Taylor, Zachary, 36–40, **39**
Texas Revolution, 33–34
Thoreau, Henry David
anarchism and, 55, 97
Brown and, 66–71
criticism of, 15–16, 49
early life, 7–8
Emerson and, 10–13, 16, 50
individualism, 47, 56–59, 61, 70–71, 95, 97
influence, 5–7, 14–15, 17, 48, 50–51, 58, 75–76, 80–83, 85, 86, 88–89, 94–97
life at Walden, 13–15
love of nature, 6, 8, 10, 17, 96
Mexican-American War and, 6–7, 17, 19–20, 48, 51–54, 58–61, 81, 86, 89, 96–97
night in jail, 6–7, 49–50, 75–76, 81, 86, 89, 94, 96–97
personality, 8, 12, 15–16
slavery and, 6–7, 17, 19–20, 48, 51–54, 58–61, 81, 86, 89, 96–97
teaching, 9–10, 16
violence and, 48, 54, 69–71
Tolstoy, Leo, 76–83, **77**, **82**, 97
transcendentalism, 11–12, 58, 71
Treaty of Guadalupe Hidalgo, 40–41, **40**
Tubman, Harriet, 62
Twin Oaks Community, 95

Walden, 13–15, 17, 95–96
Walden Two, 95
Wilmot Proviso, 41

ABOUT THE AUTHOR

Derek Miller is a writer and educator from Salisbury, Maryland. His books include *The Economy of Contemporary Africa, The Silk Road, Minority Soldiers Fighting in World War I*, and more. When he's not writing or teaching, Miller likes to hike and travel with his wife. He hopes to visit the Concord Museum's Henry David Thoreau Collection one day.